T0195901

SHAPING
YOUR
TODAY
FOR A BETTER
TOMORROW

JOHNSON F. ODESOLA

authorHOUSE®

AuthorHouse™
1663 Liberty Drive
Bloomington, IN 47403
www.authorhouse.com
Phone: 1 (800) 839-8640

Published by AuthorHouse 12/21/2019

ISBN: 978-1-7283-4083-8 (sc)
ISBN: 978-1-7283-4082-1 (e)

Print information available on the last page.

This book is printed on acid-free paper.

Scripture taken from The Holy Bible, King James Version. Public Domain

CONTENTS

CHAPTER ONE

Yesterday Begins Today

Three days exist in the human life. Yesterday which is like a stale check. Today which is like the cash in hand. And tomorrow which is like a promissory note. The human day consists of twenty four hours, no matter where you are in the globe. How you utilize your day determines your level of success in life.

Man has three days but he can only live one day at a time. Today is the day of all human activities. Nothing happens yesterday. It is in the past. Everything happens today. This is your area of strength. This should be your area of concentration.

Yesterday is gone. You can't retrieve it any more. However, you have the opportunity to make it up today. You can correct your past with your present. For example, if you failed yesterday, you can correct that impression by succeeding today. Today is your opportunity. Today is your joker.

Yesterday is gone. Forget about it. Tomorrow is yet to come. Don't fret about it. Today is what you have. Forge ahead with it to shape a better tomorrow. Listen to this, everyone has a past, a yesterday. We all have tomorrow as long as God permits. Today is our only moment of limitless opportunity.

Your today is a harvest of what you invested yesterday. Your tomorrow will be the harvest of what you are investing today. You are where you are today as a result of your actions yesterday. Where you will be tomorrow depends on your actions today.

Yesterday is gone. Your achievement of yesterday ceases to be an achievement today. It becomes history. **The realm of glory is better than the realm of history. Your yesterday is your realm of history. It is your today that is your realm of glory**. You can turn your history into glory by your actions today. It is better to live in glory than to dwell in history.

Shaping a better **tomorrow** begins **today.** Today is your leverage. Today is your opportunity to right the wrongs. It is a level playing ground for all men, no matter your level or status in life.

You can stage a comeback today
You can step up today
You can start up today
You can plant that seed today
You can dream big today
You can step out today

Step out! If you do nothing today, tomorrow will be dark and dreary. Tomorrow thrives on today. Tomorrow survives on today. **The difference between the CEO and the CLERK is in the way they made use of their 'today'**. Two people can have GM as abbreviated position. One is a General Manager while the other is a Gate Man. The difference between these GMs is in the proper and improper use of their 'today'. While the General Manager worked hard to shape his today for a better tomorrow, the Gate Man spent his day in idleness.

What you put into life is what you get out of life. If you pay the price, you will obtain the prize. Moving on to the next level is very crucial at this point in life. It doesn't matter where you are in the journey of life. There is a next level. There is a higher height and a greater glory.

The best is yet to come! The best architect is yet to display his architectural splendor. The best author is yet to write the best bestseller. The best singer is yet to sing the best song. You can be the one. You can be the next in the ladder of success.

Begin this journey of a better tomorrow by shaping your today. Look up! Look forward! The world has no place for the man that looks back. Those who look back will act back. If you engage the reverse gear of your automobile, you will certainly drag backward rather than drive forward.

Take your tomorrow today!

Your tomorrow is up to you. It is not up to the witch or wizard. It is not up to your friend or enemy. It is up to you! You owe the ace. You have the prerogative of power to shape your today for a better tomorrow. As you make your bed, so you lie on it.

You are the arbiter of your own destiny irrespective of the sinister activities of the so called 'witches' and 'wizards'. **A man is bewitched when he is far from his maker and when the garden of his mind is exposed to pests, rodents and vectors of life**. The ball is in your court! Tomorrow is up to you!

You are the arbiter of your destiny
You are the master of your life
You are the framer of your future
You are the builder of your bridge
You are the designer of your destiny
You are the architect of your life!

You possess the raw materials for the building of your today for a better tomorrow. The raw materials that build destiny include knowledge, wisdom, skills, Prayer, fasting, scriptures, discipline, vision, determination etc. God will use the raw materials you have.

When the prophet was to help the widow in 2 kings 4, he asked, 'what shall I do for thee? Tell me what hast thou in thine house?' When God was to deliver Moses and Israel from the red sea, he asked

Moses, what is that in your hand. God will use what you have as raw materials to shape your destiny.

> 'And i will give unto thee the keys of the kingdom of
> heaven: and whatsoever thou shalt bind on earth shall
> be bound in heaven: and whatsoever thou shalt loose
> on earth shall be loosed in heaven'- Matt. 16:19

You have the keys. You have the prerogative of power to shape an enviable destiny. Telling God to do what you are required to do is praying amiss. Multitudes of Christians pray amiss. It is like asking God to dress your bed upon rising from sleep in the morning. That's your prerogative! God will not help you to wash your kitchen utensils. That's your job! He will not mow your lawn. It's up to you!

There are certain responsibilities you must carry out in your life journey. Shaping your today for a better tomorrow is like a two way traffic.

1. What God needs to do
2. What you need to do

God and you are the only partners in this business of destiny building. You are the principal partner. You are the major stakeholder in the business of your life. If you are bankrupt, you will find yourself to blame.

God in his goodness has given us a pattern in the bible that will help us to shape our tomorrow. The book of Genesis clearly reveals to us how he shaped our today.

> 'And the earth was without form and void; and darkness
> was upon the face of the face of the deep...'- Gen.1:2

When God shaped the world in which we live today, there was no land. There were no sun, moon and stars. There were no aquatic or land animals. Man was not in existence.

We are beneficiaries of his creative prowess today. We use water as our universal solvent. The sun, moon and stars give us natural light. The sun generates heat that we require for temperature balance. We have plant and animal food. And so much more!

God shaped our world by taking deliberate and concrete steps. He did not wish things to happen like people do today. He followed a pattern in his recreation.

> *'Through faith we understand that the worlds were framed by the word of God, so that the things which are seen were not made of things which do appear'*-
> Heb. 11:3

The creative ability of God resides in you. You have the nature and likeness of God. You are complete in him! There is an inherent power and ability of God in you. Like God the father, you can shape a colorful world around you.

> *'But as many as believed him to them gave he power to become the sons of God, even to them that believed on his name,-* John 1:12

> *'Ye are of God little children, and have overcome them: because greater is he that is in you than he that is in the world'-* 1 John 4:4

Jesus demonstrated divine abilities, the abilities of God. He excelled in ministry. He healed the sick, raised the dead, cast out demons and set the captives free.

That same ability of God is in you. You should be a chip of the old block. God laced you with creative abilities when he created you. You can rule your world. You can fulfill your dreams, hope and aspirations.

> *'How God anointed Jesus of Nazareth with the Holy Ghost and with power: who went about doing good*

*and healing all that were oppressed of the devil ; for
God was with him'*- Acts 10:38

God is with you too. Jesus was the express image of God when
he walked and worked on earth. He manifested the grace and glory
of God. That's what God is expecting us to do: to manifest his grace
and glory.

> *'For the earnest expectation of the creature waiteth
> for the manifestation of the sons of God'*- Rom. 8:19

- You can shape your today for a better tomorrow. God is in you- 1 John 4:4
- You can shape your today for a better tomorrow. God is for you- Rom. 8:31
- You can shape your today for a better tomorrow. God is with you- Matt.1:23

TWO

God's pattern # 1: Planning

The word 'plan' means *a set of intended actions, usually mutually related, through which one expects to achieve a goal.* It is a set of program towards a specific goal. It is an action graph; an arrangement of carefully drawn out steps in order to fulfill an ultimate desire.

To fail to plan is already a plan to fail. Great people are astute planners. They succeed before they begin by putting up an excellent plan and action procedure.

The greatest example of an excellent planner is God. God is a God of plan and action. He is always steps ahead. See how he planned and created the world in six days!

> He put light in place first of all in the recreation- Gen. 1:3
> He separated the waters from the waters by the firmament- Gen. 1:6-7
> He created the land from the waters and called it earth Gen. 1:9-10
> He caused the earth to bring forth plants for food and herbs- Gen. 1:12
> He created animals that live in the sea, land and fly in the air - Gen. 1:20-25
> He made man after his image and likeness and blessed him- Gen. 1:26-28

There is no better plan that can be put in place than this. Everything was in place before the arrival of Adam. When he arrived, he had no lack. The sun was in place to give him heat and light in the day. The moon and stars were already here to give him light at night. The sea animals were in abundance to give him meat and animal protein. The plants were in place to give him food and herbs. The Garden of Eden was a one stop shop. Everything man needed for survival was provided.

And when it was time to provide a partner; a soulmate for Adam, he put him to a deep sleep and brought a rib out of him with which he made the woman. To test the creative ability he put in man, God told Adam to name all the animals. He accurately did. He called the human God made out of his rib woman. What a perfect God he is! What a perfect planner!

1. He did not create man and then remember to provide the food and herbs man will need.
2. He did not create man and then discovered that he would need sun for heat in the garden which was a vast expanse.
3. He did not create the woman for the man and afterwards looked for a way to provide the means for the man to cater for her.
4. He did not create Adam and Eve and put them in the sea.
5. He did not create man and his wife and put them in darkness.

God is a master planner. He is infallible in his plans. He is proficient in putting the right pegs in the right holes. He does every 'i' and crosses every't'. He plans for contingencies. He has remedial provisions for his master plan.

Adam and Eve fell from grace in the garden. They were naked upon eating the forbidden fruit. But God already made provision for their clothing. Animal skin was handy. Adam and Eve died spiritually when they ate the fruit. God already provided a remedy in the second Adam, Jesus Christ, the Lamb of God which was slain before the foundation of the world.

- God planned it: the death of Jesus on the tree to take away the death penalty of mankind.
- God planned it: the salvation of man before he was lost.
- God planned it: forgiveness of sin before man committed the sin.

God is a master planner.

✓ His plans are impeccable.
✓ His purpose is eternal.
✓ His steps are infallible.

Manifest God's planning ability

People see the devil as an obstacle. It is correct that Satan and his cohorts are real but they are not powerful enough to truncate your tomorrow if you do what is expected of you to do. They cannot subdue your destiny if you follow the pattern of God for your life.

It is not so much of the externals: enemies, demons, circumstances etc that are against you. It is rather so much of what you do with the pattern of God for your life.

An American judge said: 'obstacles without are tiny matters compared to obstacles within'. The major obstacle to your success in life is that which is within: you. **You are the only obstacle to your life. Whatever the human mind can conceive and believe he can achieve**. His limitation is that which he permits.

God is Omnipotent, Omnipresent and Omniscient. You can link your impotence with his Omnipotence. **He is Sovereign. You can terminate your suffering by hooking up with his sovereignty**. Apostle Paul acknowledged this:

'I can do all things through Christ that strengthens me- Phil. 4:13

There is something wrong somewhere when things are not in their proper perspective. It is certainly not with God. Check it out.

We have established the fact that God is perfect. He is infallible and righteous. His plans for you are good and not evil, to give you a future and hope.

The devil does not have power over you especially if you are a believer in Christ. He cannot compel or control your life. Now if the problem is not with God and certainly not with Satan, for he does not have authority over you, it is certainly with you!

You are the clog in the wheel of your destiny. As you lay your bed, so you lie on it! You constitute a clog to your tomorrow when you refuse to plan. **You become the enemy of your tomorrow when you live without a definite plan. You form a barrier to puncture your future when you are planless!**

God is a Master Planner. He is our pattern, yardstick or plumb line. Follow his steps as the Model Master Planner. Don't just approach life with levity. To get the best out of life, you need to plan. You can obtain your portion of the master plan of God by going back to the original master planner. He has the blueprint. Go for it!

You need to be original. Don't follow the bandwagon. It is not everything people do that you should do. Get the original copy of God's plan for your life. You are unique. You are peculiar. There is nobody exactly like you of the more than seven billion people on earth.

You are not an illegitimate being. You did not arrive here on earth accidentally. **You are not merely a product of your parents' copulation. No, God planned your arrival**. He spent more than seven months molding you in your mother's womb.

There is something special about you. Only God has the details. Get the pattern for your life from God. Moses got and built according to the pattern God showed him in the mount. You need to know God's plan, purpose and program for your life! Morris Cerulo said: 'God is a God of plan, purpose and objectivity'.

Plan around God's purpose for you

You can't be jack of all trades. There is a particular pattern that is designed for you. There is a line you must tow in order for you to arrive at a certain destination. **If you tow no line, you will arrive nowhere. There are several people who are going no where**.

> *'For this purpose the son of God was manifested, that he might destroy the works of the devil'*- 1 John 3:8

Jesus knew the purpose of his life here on earth. That was why he set out at the age of twelve. Joseph and Mary found him in the temple, reasoning with the doctors of law. And when they queried his action, he said to them: *'How is it that ye sought me? Wist ye not that I must be about my father's business'*-Luke 2:49

In other words, you didn't need to look for me! You should have known where to find me: in the temple. You should have known that I must be doing the will of God and following his plan and pattern for my life!

At the age of twelve, Jesus knew he was headed towards cavalry. He was in the picture of the plan and purpose of God.

He knew the will of God: *'my meat is to do the will of him that sent me and finish his work'*- John 4:34

He approached the purpose for his life with uttermost urgency: *'I must work the works of him that sent me while it is day, for the night cometh when no man can work'*- John 9:4

He carried out his life assignment to the finish line: *I have glorified thee on the earth: I have finished the work which thou gavest me to do'*- John 17:4

He cried out at the finish line: *'It is finished'*- John 19:30

Look at the pattern Jesus followed! He discovered and pursued purpose by adequate planning. He planned his evangelistic campaigns. He strategically located himself besides the well of Jacob to reach and turn around the life of the Samaritan. Her life drew other people to the kingdom afterwards.

He planned his last supper in the upper room. He planned his triumphal entry into Jerusalem. The life and ministry of our Lord, Jesus Christ followed the pattern of God. This greatly accounted for his success in all ramifications.

There is a divine pattern for animals: eat, sleep, wake up, procreate. That's all. You can't follow that pattern. You are not one of those animals in the animal kingdom. There is much more to life than to eat, sleep, wake up and procreate. There is a purpose for your life. There is a reason why you are here.

> *'Before I formed thee in the belly, I knew thee; and before thou camest forth out of the womb, I sanctified thee, and I ordained thee a prophet unto the nations'-* Jeremiah 1:5

There was something back of the mind of God when he created Jerry. It was the prerogative of Jeremiah to align himself with this purpose and pursue it to a logical end.

You are on a mission here on earth. Find it out and write your mission statement boldly and clearly. You have an assignment to fulfill. You are an answer to certain questions and solution to certain problems.

Develop a plan to carry out your life mission. Don't just work for the sake of working. Map out a plan to achieve a worthwhile goal. **Plan your work and work out your plan**. Get to the bottom of what, why, how to do the things you are cut out to do.

Do you want to marry? **Why** do you want to marry? **When** do you want to marry? **Who** do you want to marry? **How** do you want to marry? **Where** do you want to marry? Do you want to have children? Follow the same pattern of concrete plan.

Ask yourself: why am I doing what I am doing? What must I do to achieve the set goal? What price must I pay to obtain the prize? What improvements must I seek? Put a good plan in place before doing anything in life.

A certain man in West Africa won a lottery. He searched for

what to do with the money but couldn't find one. ***It is better to have a plan in place before the resources come***. This man had no plan. And here was money!

Not knowing what to do with the money, he aggravated his condition by wooing and taking the last wife of a popular millionaire in the country. News got to this polygamist money bag that the young man that just won a lottery is keeping his last wife. The lottery prize was $50, 000. The rich man simply sued him for $50, 000 with some extra charges!

Plan and plan well. This young man lost his lottery money because he did not have a plan. Some people have no plan. They quite easily play the ball in the courts of God. When you ask them about their tomorrow, they will say, '*I don't know, it is in the hand of God*'.

Stop passing the bulk! The ball is in your court! Have a plan for tomorrow. Plan your life under the leading of the Holy Spirit. Some people are completely oblivious about their life. They don't have the foggiest idea of what to do. Now, if you don't know what to do, get back to God. He has a plan for you.

Get serious about life and carve out a definite plan to succeed. As a student, for example, plan your course of study. Plan your study pattern. Have a specific grade target. Go the extra mile to prepare for your exams and put in your best in every question before you.

Fasting, praying and reading the bible will not fetch you the grade you want. It is a good thing to fast and pray. It is ideal to read the bible. But having good grades will not come by fasting and praying. You need to develop a study pattern to cover your syllabus thoroughly with implicit understanding. You may have to burn the midnight candles.

> ➢ Plan well. Every great achiever planned well.
> ➢ Plan as a father or mother- the home will be a haven on earth.
> ➢ Plan as a student- you will succeed in your academics.
> ➢ Plan as an employee- you will excel in your duties.
> ➢ Plan as a job seeker- you will be gainfully employed.

- ➢ Plan as a spinster- you will meet the right man to walk with you down the aisle.
- ➢ Plan as a bachelor- you will find a gracious damsel to tie the nuptial cord with.
- ➢ Plan as a newlywed- you will experience an endless marital bliss.
- ➢ Plan as a pastor- you will have a healthy and buoyant congregation.

In all you do, plan properly. Don't live anything on chance. Life is a matter of choice and not chance. Do what is required of you. And don't defer to tomorrow what you can do today!

CHAPTER THREE

God's pattern # 2: Wisdom

Wisdom is vital to shaping your today for a better tomorrow. It is in indispensable key to destiny molding. God has made enough provision for us according to the scriptures.

> *'If any of you lack wisdom, let him ask of God, that giveth to all men liberally, and upbraideth not; and it shall be given you'*- James 1:5

God is magnanimous with wisdom. He gives it liberally to those who desire it. There is no price too high to pay in order to get it. There is no sacrifice too much In exchange. Those who cherish it like pure gold know its value and that's why they can give everything to possess it.

> *'Get wisdom, get understanding: forget it not neither decline from the words of my mouth. Forsake her not and she shall preserve thee: live her, and she shall keep thee. Wisdom is the principal thing; therefore, get wisdom: and with all thy getting, get understanding'*- Proverbs 4:5-7

There are several born again Christians who live in foolishness. Blood washed, heaven bound, Holy Ghost filled and tongue talking but grossly lack wisdom. God will empower you with skills, knowledge and abilities but you will need wisdom to properly channel your endowment.

Having power, skill or ability without wisdom is like giving a gun to an untrained soldier. He will kill everybody around including himself. You don't give a jet to an amateur to fly. He will kill every passenger on board. The half-baked captain will sink the ship and the baby chauffeur will veer off the road and crash the car against a tree.

This is what happens without wisdom. Destinies are truncated, visions are subdued, purposes are unfulfilled and goals are unreached. There is the need for proper instruction and information on 'how to'. It is not enough to know what to do or have a vision. You need to know how to execute it.

Wisdom is living in light. Without wisdom, it is like groping in darkness like a moth. Don't live another day without wisdom. Those who lack wisdom have no light to guide their feet. They will fumble, stumble and crumble in the long run. Live in the light, the wisdom of God.

In the shaping of your today for a better tomorrow, wisdom will shed light to life threatening problems and proffer an impeccable panacea. Your tomorrow will certainly be better in Jesus name! Seek wisdom. Be an answer to questions of men. Be a solutions to problems of the society. You need wisdom to give you this leverage and bring you above board.

How did Joseph get out of Pharaoh's dungeon? By wisdom! First, he interpreted the butler and baker's dreams. And then, he interpreted Pharaoh's dream and proffered the solution to avoid the national calamity the dream portends.

Joseph solved the life threatening problem of a nation. Wisdom was the key. He answered the question of national economic security. **May God give you wisdom to excel in life and ministry. May foolishness be far from your life and family in Jesus name!**

I speak into your life right now, may you be a custodian of the wisdom that comes from above in Jesus name! May answers to human questions drop at your fingertips. May solutions to problems of men crop up in your finite mind in Jesus mighty name!

You will not lack wisdom. You will not be bankrupt of ideas and revelations. You will not grope in darkness. I stand in the authority in the name of the Lord to prophesy triumph for you in life threatening issues. You will emerge victorious. You will be celebrated and not tolerated. You will jump out of the valley of defeat to the height of victory.

In the process of building a good tomorrow by shaping today, wisdom will provide you the skill to evade traps and pitfalls. It will make you take prompt and proper decisions. It will keep you out of troubles. Some people back out when they face oppositions. Wisdom will help you navigate your way through the rough and tough terrains of life. If you don't give up, you will get up. **Wisdom provides the ability to stand face to face with challenges, pop up ideas in your imaginative and creative faculty and resolve difficult issues**. When you approach life in wisdom, you will enjoy lasting progress and peace.

A legend was told about a red hunter (names.........................) who went hunting. He couldn't get any animal to kill that day of his adventure. On his way home from the field, he saw a sparrow. He threw his bait and caught the sparrow. At least, he was not going home without a catch.

The sparrow pleaded to the hunter not to kill him. He said: *'Please, hunter, don't kill me. I have three piece of advice for you'.* The hunter was all ears.

1. *Don't regret any good thing you do.*
2. *Don't believe any word that does not have root in the book of the creator.*
3. *Don't use artificial lifter to lift anything up. Live a normal life and ask of the help of people who are taller than you.*

The three piece of advice looked pleasant in the eyes of the hunter. He released the poor bird who flew to the next tree and said: *'foolish hunter, foolish hunter, I have gold and diamond in my belly. Foolish hunter.*

The hunter was perplexed at the trick of the tiny little creature. In his reaction, he negated the three piece of the sparrow's advice.

Don't regret any good thing you do. Releasing the sparrow was a good thing. The hunter regretted His action. He wished he had him, perhaps because his belly was a house of gold and diamond.

Don't believe any word that does not have root in the book of the creator. The hunter believed there was gold and diamond in the belly of the sparrow without tracing it to the book of the creator. He negated the second piece of advice by his belief.

Don't use artificial lifter to lift anything up. Live a normal life and ask of the help of people who are taller than you. In rage, the hunter started climbing the tree in pursuit of the sparrow. He fell down from a tender branch in the process.

The sparrow was not done yet. He flew close to the helpless hunter who was wriggling in excruciating pain and spoke in his ears:

'foolish hunter, foolish hunter. I gave you three piece of advice and you violated all of them, foolish hunter, foolish hunter, may your soul rest in peace'.

The hunter was truly foolish. If he was wise, he would have kept the sparrow as meat for his belly. He wouldn't have regretted doing good according to the sparrow. And he certainly wouldn't have fallen for a cheap lie that the sparrow's tiny belly had gold and diamond.

Wisdom is principal in life

You need wisdom to lead a good life. People who lack wisdom in their daily living will have enough hard nuts to crack. They will find many hurdles in life that are frustrating. Oh, they will meet with brick and impregnable walls. In the build up towards a better tomorrow, you will associate with people of all cadres and calibers.

You will meet detractors and pessimists. You will come across dream killers. Your association will not be devoid of mean minds who do not know what life is all about. There will be enemies of progress on the way. You will find betrayers in your company.

How you handle people and events will depend on the reading in your wisdom- o- meter. How equipped with wisdom you are will matter a lot in your dealings. No man is an island. No man is a compendium of knowledge. You can not live in isolation.

It is wisdom to forgive others. Some people are terrible in their ways. The more you forgive, the worst things they do to hurt you. They may seem not to deserve pardon but it is wisdom to still forgive them. If you forgive men their trespasses, God will forgive you your trespasses too. Lack of forgiveness hinders prayers. That's why it is wisdom to forgive people. You are helping yourself to shape a better tomorrow if you do.

It is wisdom to bless others. There are people who behave like a dead sea. They only take but never give. They withhold their tithes and offerings. They refrain from sowing seeds in the ministry and lives of others who are in need. They are covetous in disposition. Those who are wise know that the liberal soul shall be made fat. They are aware that it is more blessed to give than to receive.

It is wisdom to fast and pray. God enjoins us in scriptures to fast and pray. This world in which we live is as much spiritual as it is physical. Jesus gave us a standing example. He prayed a great while before it was day. His life and ministry was characterized by fervent prayers. The garden of Gethsemane was his usual resort. That was where he rounded up his ministry before he went to the cross.

You cannot shape your today for a better tomorrow without adequate and fervent prayers. That's the master key to all closed doors. Ask and you shall be given. Seek and you shall find. Knock and it shall be opened unto you. Jesus said to always pray and not faint. Apostle Paul enjoined us to pray without ceasing.

You cannot dispense with prayers in the shaping of a better tomorrow. They that wait upon the Lord shall renew their strength. They are the group of people that will not wear out in their pursuit. They will never faint in the way. Wisdom demands that you carve out your moments of fasting and prayer. You need it to triumph in this wicked world!

It is wisdom to dwell peaceably with your spouse. *'Likewise ye husbands, dwell with tnem according to knowledge, giving honour to your wife, as unto the weaker vessel, and as being heirs together of the grace of life; that your prayers be not hindered'*-1pet.2:17.

Marriage is a sacred institution. The bible says it is honorable. It is a life journey; a sacred trust. It is a vow and sacrifice that must be preserved. Those who are wise protect this institution with utmost commitment.

Be wise and be content with the wife of your youth. Stay glued to your spouse with a strong adherence. Let peace reign in your family and make it a no go zone for the devil. **Run a successful home in order to run a successful business, ministry or career**. Charity, they say, begins at home. Let your home be a beacon of light. Make it a haven of comfort and peace. Then, your tomorrow shall receive a boost that money cannot procure or bequeath.

Wisdom is principal in life and ministry. In life, there are difficult human beings who will stand akimbo to dull your wits and cancel your courage. It takes wisdom to deal with such people. They may be distant or close alleys. Wisdom is essential in overcoming the human angle of challenges.

It is not stupidity to show love in the midst of hate. **Jesus had enemies all around him. But he discomfited them by the virtue of love. Love is an unbeatable weapon in the hands of a believer**. It is the last straw that breaks the Carmel's back. Wisdom will make you exhibit love in the midst of hate.

A woman was continually haunted by a wicked soul. In fury for vengeance, she prayed fire and brimstone to edge out this man. All manners of fiery prayer proved abortive. This went on for eight years. She was under extreme torment until she met a man of God who told her to engage the mystery of love to dislodge the powers of the devilish man.

At first, she shrieked in defiance. Meanwhile, attacks from the evil messenger continued. She decided to obey the man of God and started blessing her enemy rather than sending fire and brimstone which had failed for eight uninterrupted years. Rather than fire, she was sending money to the man. The man died four months later. Within four months, love conquered an enemy vengeance could not stop for eight years!

> 'Recompense to no man evil for evil...avenge not yourselves, but rather give place unto wrath: for it is written, vengeance is mine; I will repay, saith the Lord. Therefore if thine enemy hunger, feed him; if he thirst, give him drink: for in so doing thou shalt heap coals of fire on his head- Romans 12:17-20

That was what the woman did by wisdom. She heaped a coal of fire on her enemy's head by showing love instead of hate. Wisdom teaches love in the midst of hate. **Frustrate the counsel of the enemy by walking in love. There is power in walking in the love of God.**

Those who are wise will patiently uproot evil structures on their way to fulfillment in life and ministry. They will do the will God. They will obey the word of God. And they will go the way of God.

Those who are wise will be committed to the work of the kingdom of God. If you care less about the things of God, you are putting a lid on your tomorrow. God is committed to those who are committed to his kingdom. You cannot be nonchalant and expect the blessings of God to drop on your laps. It is wisdom to be useful in the kingdom works.

Those who are wise win souls. *'He that winneth soul is wise'.* Soul winning is not the prerogative of the evangelists. It is not the exclusive job of the pastor, teacher, prophet or apostle. It is the collective responsibility of every believer. It takes wisdom to take this responsibility personal. Are you a soul winner? Be wise. Be on the go to fish out souls for the Master.

Where ever you are, whatever you do, soul winning is our collective job. As a medical doctor, for example, your primary assignment is not to treat the patients. That is secondary. Your primary assignment is to show and share the love of God. You are an ambassador of Christ anywhere any day.

Whatever your profession is, make sure to show and share the love of God. It is your primary duty if you truly know the Lord. He saved you that you might serve him. He showed you the way that you might show others the way. **Be wise. Spread the good news! Go a fishing as a regular routine**.

A word for the youths

Listen to me young ones, choose wisdom that you may excel in life. **Life is a process. It is not lived from the top but from the bottom upwards.** This generation of indomie expectations will not survive the true test of faith in God. The world has become a place of instant breakthrough. No wonder several people are breaking down.

Dearly beloved young ones, avoid shortcuts. Avoid the abracadabra way. Choose the right way and method in all you do. Let the Holy Spirit be your constant guide. Run away from the way of Balaam. This prophet wanted quick gratifications. God had to choose a donkey to speak to him to desist from his carnal pursuit.

There is a way that seems right unto a man but it leads to destruction. **Shortcuts can cut the life of a person short. That's why it's called shortcut. It is capable of cutting short the life, glory and destiny of the fool.** Sometimes, the shortest cut turns out to be the longest route. Why would you waste your time, energy and resources only to find out how foolish you are in the long run.

Choose the right way all the time. People make excuses for not doing the right thing. Those that despise instructions device destruction for themselves. Remember all that glitter is not gold. Don't be Penny wise and pound foolish. Put the right pegs in the right holes.

As much as you can, look kempt. Look good. Smell good. Be merry, don't be moody or gloomy. **Wearing a long face will reduce your facial value and repel people from you**. Be glad don't be sad. Be merry, don't be moody.

Do you want a husband? Look young. No man will marry a mama. **Dress well and smart. Be decently trendy**. Get into the youth bracket in your appearance. Someone said you will be addressed the way you are dressed. Don't look forty when you are only twenty five.

Do you want a wife? Clean up! **Smell good. Use Cologne and freshen up your appearance**. Visit a dentist, at least, once in a year to sanitize your dentition. Leave your haircut alluring. Don't be idle. Get something going on for you. Adam was already tilling the ground when Eve arrived. Be busy doing what will boost your economy.

Some people dig their grave with their teeth. They eat just about any junk they find. Eat well. Avoid red meat to an extent especially when you are above forty. You need to be alive to have a better tomorrow. Check your sugar intake. Control your fries and cholesterol.

Eat to live rather than live to eat. Some people live to eat. They have no control over their appetite. Their belly is their god. Put a knife to your throat my friend and restrain yourself from eating like a maggot. Human beings are not supposed to chew the cord like cows.

And then, be fit. Have a procedure for exercise. Inculcate the habit of medical checkup. Take enough time to rest when it is necessary. If the horse dies the work will be continued by another horse. May the Lord grant you wisdom in all you do.

FOUR

God's pattern # 3: Have A Vision

In 1968, when I was in primary five in a dingy school, one of my cousins came from Italy to Nigeria. Life in those days aren't the same today. He wore a shoe called stiletto. That was in the vogue then. The sound that followed each step he took particularly fascinated me.

Curious, I asked my father who the young man was. 'He is your cousin from Italy, my father answered. Still curious, I asked, 'what does he do?' My father answered, 'he is an engineer. He just arrived from Italy to visit with us.

That was it! I wanted to be an engineer. After my secondary school, I told my father I want to study engineering like my cousin. He didn't like the idea any bit. He wanted me to inherit his sawmill business. But I insisted to study engineering, pointing him to the fact that he didn't inherit his father's business, so I was not obliged to inherit his too.

Again, my position did not go down well with my father. That was where the battle line was drawn. Even though I did not know what it was to be an engineer at that time, I wanted to be one at all cost. That was a clearly defined vision. I was ready to stake all to take all.

My father did not compromise. His position was that I must join him in the sawmill business. I did not compromise either. An engineer, come what may. He was not going to bulge until I rescind my decision. So, he abandoned the issue of my career for an interminable length of time.

My daily routine was simple: go out to play football, come back, eat and sleep. This continued for a long time until he called me one day and said to me with a conclusive voice of authority : 'son, go to the sawmill. I have already drafted you as the director of the business. So, get down to work!'

My answer was stern and firm. I will never work as a sawmill director. Head or tail, I must be an engineer. My father calmly walked away disappointed. He made an appointment for me to meet a counsellor who he already briefed to talk me out of my dream or vision. His efforts too to convince me to drop my idea and choose the sawmill proved abortive.

I don't know how it happened, but by a clandestine and subtle arrangement, I was put as an apprentice under somebody, a bricklayer. Remember I told you that I didn't know what it meant to be an engineer. In my naivety, I thought I was in an engineering school.

After four years as an apprentice, I was issued a certificate. Bravo! I am an engineer! In excitement, I applied to several companies as an engineer, each time enclosing my certificate, a bricklaying certificate. All my effort to get a job was futile.

One day, a bearded man called and interacted with me. That was the day I discovered my plight. He asked me, 'do you know who you are?' I said yes, 'I am an engineer. He laughed jestingly and said, 'no, you are not an engineer, you are a bricklayer.

That was bombshell! Right there, I brought out the certificate and tore it into shreds. I cried profusely when I got home. But I was resolute to be an engineer. My mind was made up. There was no going back. In my resilience, I went ahead to qualify to study engineering in the university. Before I graduated, I got a job. It happened that I solved a problem for an Italian engineering company which hired me afterwards. While still in school!

Failure is not final. That you failed an exam or in business does not make you a failure. **You are a failure only when you quit trying to succeed**. Thomas Edison failed ten thousand times in the development of the incandescent lamp. That didn't make him a failure. He simply concluded that he found ten thousand ways it wouldn't work! He found that one way to make it work eventually.

Get a vision and stand by it. Don't sit before the television all your life! Those you watch have their vision. That's why they are celebrated. That's why you are watching them. You too can be watched in the television. **Get a vision if you want to be watched in the television!**

You are not created to roam about in life. You have a place in God's grand plan. The amplified version of the bible says: 'I know the thoughts and plans I have for you, says the Lord, thoughts and plans for welfare and peace and not for evil, to give you hope in your final outcome'- Jeremiah 29:11

Locate your place in the master plan of God by vision. **There is a future and hope for you. Get a vision to arrive at this future and hope. Vision is an ideal or goal towards which one aspires.** You cannot be fulfilled in life if you lack a clear vision. Several people lack vision. They have eyes but cannot see far into tomorrow.

Helen Keller said about vision: The most pathetic person in the world is someone who has sight without vision. The only thing worse than being blind is having sight but no vision.

It may interest you to know that Helen Keller became blind and deaf shortly after birth. But in spite of her misfortunes, she had her name written in the pages of the history of great people. She simply had a vision even though she was blind and deaf.

Joel 2:28 tells us that the young men shall see visions. Do you have one? Abraham had a vision at the age of 75. Caleb wanted the mountain to overcome and occupy at 85. His strength was not abated after 40 years of sojourn. He had the strength of a youth.

It doesn't matter how old you are. You can still develop a vision. **Don't let your age cage you. You are not too old to dream big and pursue your dream to logical fulfillment.** You are not too young either. Samuel had a vision at a tender age. God called and gave him a specific assignment which was fulfilled in his latter years. Rise up today and prayerfully locate a worthwhile vision.

People back and black out quite easily because they don't have a vision back of their endeavors. Those who quit do so for lack of vision. And people don't quit because they fail. They rather fail because they quit.

> *'Where there is no vision, the people perish'*
> - Proverbs 29:18

That's why people quit! Lack of vision. It is so sad how people live in mediocrity as if life is all about food, clothing and shelter. There is no drive. There is no plan, purpose and pursuit. Nothing propels them. Nothing is at stake for them. Day in day out, they live as though life will never end on earth.

What's your vision?
What's your passion?
What do you seek to achieve in the short and long run?
Where do you see yourself in the next five, ten or twenty years?
What impact do you seek to make on people?
What's your drive and concern towards the kingdom?

There is a world of difference between vision and ambition. Most people are ambitious. They are not visionaries. Ambition is what you want to achieve. Vision is what God wired you for. It is God's plan and purpose for you. Develop a vision, not ambition. Ambition is dangerous when God is not in it. Absalom was ambitious. He got killed in the process.

No one makes meaningful progress in life without vision. The difference between successful people and failures is vision. Vision is like a traveler in a vehicle on a journey. He has a destination and he will reach there no matter how long it takes. People who have no vision have nowhere as destination. It is like what is known as *'Agbero'* in Nigeria.

The Agberos work in the car park. They solicit for travelers to enter the vehicle going to particular locations in the country. They help in the haulage of the passengers' luggage. Once the passengers are seated and the car has the number of required people, they move on to the next empty vehicle and solicit for passengers. They never travel out of the car park.

There are people who can be likened to the 'Agberos'. They go nowhere but merely get fallouts or handouts for survival. They lack vision, hence have no destination in view. Daily survival is the zenith in their myopic view. **They are mental pigmies who have no height advantage.**

Do you have a vision? Get on the next level. Don't be a local champion. God wants you to be a global figure. The earnest expectation of the creature waiteth for the manifestation of the sons of God- Romans 819. The entire world is waiting for you to manifest the glory of God. The world is waiting for the display of your skill, prowess, spiritual and mental ability.

So, don't localize your vision. Globalize it. Raise your vision level. Get it out of the personal trinity level: 'I, me, and myself. Let your vision transcend you. Let it be people oriented vision. Let it be a vision that cuts across people, races, gender and nations.

CHAPTER FIVE

God's pattern # 4: Keep Your Focus

Every height you see is attainable with God. The scripture is very clear on this: *'for with God nothing shall be impossible'*- Luke 1:37. There is no limitation to human achievement except that which the mind acknowledges and accepts.

God had to do something to stop the inhabitants if babel in their bid to build a tower that will reach the sky. The definiteness of their vision, plan and wisdom was inexplicable. Their unflinching determination and bulldog persistence was unbeatable. Nothing will stop them in their indestructible focus to build a tower to reach God.

God said: *'Behold these people are one, and they have one language; and this they begin to do: and now nothing will be restrained from them, which they have imagined to do'*- Gen.11:6

This was God's submission. Nothing will be able to stop them from implementing their vision of building a tower up to the heavens. **Truly, man can achieve what he conceives and believes, irrespective of obstacles.** The key is focus; unflinching determination and concentrated effort.

God knows the unstoppable power he built in the human mind. Adam demonstrated his latent and innate ability by giving names accurately to all the creatures God created. The human mind is rich! **There is more wealth in the mind than in the bank. There is more gold in the human mind than in the goldmines of South Africa.**

Yes, there is more oil in the human mind than in the oil fields of Kuwait.

God had to scatter the people by distorting their language in order to stop them from their definite desire. Nothing will stop a man of focus from achieving his goal. Not humanic demons. Not Satan himself! **Man is unstoppable if he truly has a vision and he is ready to focus on his goal until fulfillment.**

Try it out with a hammer on a rock. The first time you hit the rock with the hammer is not when the rock shatters into splinters. And if you hit point A and then move to hit point B, C, D and so on, you will never break the rock. But if you focus on one spot and continue to hit it with the hammer, the rock will break eventually.

That is the power of focus. Life is not hit and run. You need to maintain a proper and steady focus on your worthwhile goal in order to achieve it. **If you don't give up, you will get up.** Robert Schuller said: *'Tough times never last but tough people do'.*

Listen to me, dearly beloved, when it is rough, be tough. When it is tough, keep up keeping on. Tough times never really last. Only tough people do. Ice will always thaw with time. Hot water will ultimately come down to normal temperature with time. Don't give up your dreams. Don't lose your vision. Keep your eyes on your goal.

Athletes who go for gold have this habit of focus. Their eyes are always fixed on the gold. They will not give in to any distraction. The terrain could be tough and rough but one thing uppermost in their mind is the gold in the offing.

The power of focus is enormous. **Concentrate your efforts in what you do and you will get results at the appropriate time.** Don't quit. People who quit never win. Fight to finish. People who give up too soon ultimately lose the glory in the story. They lose it before they reach it.

Napoleon Hill tells a story of a young man, an uncle of Mr. R U Darby, who lost his focus. He quit too soon when he was close to victory. It was in the gold-rush days. Like other people, he went west to dig for gold.

Days and weeks of strenuous efforts to get gold in the mines went by until he discovered some shinny ore. That was a clear indication that there was gold beneath. Uncle took proper steps upon this discovery. First, he quietly covered up the source of the shinny ore and travelled back to his home in Williamsburg, Maryland and told some of his relatives about the discovery. They got money together and procured the needed equipment to dig for gold and get rich.

The discovery of the shinny ore proved that Darby and his uncle were in for the big killing in profits as the first consignment of the material was analyzed to be one the best in the mines of Colorado. So, they continued the search with the shipped equipment until the traces of gold in the mines disappeared.

No man is ever defeated until he quits. Failure is not final. It is only a temporary defeat. Darby and his uncle would soon learn this truth in a hard way. They dug until they were convinced that there was no more gold. Disappointed, they quit, sold their equipment to another fellow and took the next available train back to Williamsburg.

People start hot when they venture into their dreams but gradually lose steam and back out when they are stretched out of their wits. **You are close to victory when you are most apt to quit**. Darby and his uncle did not know this. That's why they quit, gave up their burning desire and retracted.

The man that purchased the mining equipment went to the field in the company of an expert, a mining engineer and demanded onsite assessment of the mines. The expert's result showed that the Darbys were three feet away from gold, real gold when they sold their equipment. That was the truth. The man dug only three feet into the mines and hit the gold zone. He made millions of dollars in ore.

If you lose your focus, you will forfeit the fortune. Only three feet from gold! If only they hit the soil a few more times. If only they struck the mines a few more times. Someone will continue from where your vision stops and emerge a champion. Someone will pick up the remains of your dream and rise up to unprecedented heights. The difference is only three feet away. Stay in until you hit the gold zone. Don't ever give up your vision.

Darby and his uncle learnt a valuable lesson a hard way. The lesson turned out to be a blessing to Darby when he went into insurance business. He had learnt to stay focused until light breaks forth. He would not stop three feet away from victory any more.

He remembered his experience in the Colorado mines each time he stood before clients in his life insurance business. He would always say to himself: '*I stopped three feet from gold, but I will never stop because men say NO when I ask them to buy insurance*'. He had learnt that there is always a YES behind a NO.

Focus is an incredible force for accomplishment. Jesus, our Lord and Master achieved his mission with irresistible focus. He set his face like a flint towards the purpose of his life on earth. The bible says about him: '*The zeal of thine house hath eaten me up*'- John 2:17

Focus is a driving force propelled by zeal. It is an essential virtue for accomplishment. Defeat will certainly rear up its ugly head but focus will push you on in spite of odds. It makes you see the end from the beginning. It makes you see the glory ahead.

> '*Looking unto Jesus the author and finisher of our faith; who for the joy that was set before him endured the cross, despising the shame, and is set down at the right hand of God*'- Hebrews 12:2

Focus makes you see the joy of success way ahead. It makes you consider the end from the beginning. It motivates giant and bold steps, stirs up your imaginative and creative faculty, puts off discouragement and helps you concentrate your attention on the goal.

That was the virtue that kept Apostle Paul on his feet. No threat from the religious gladiators of his days could deter him from preaching the gospel. He said: '*woe is unto me if I preach not the gospel*'- 1 Cor. 9:16. He was ready to go to Jerusalem in jeopardy of his life when prophet Agabus warned him of the impending doom.

What was the sole desire of his heart? To see the salvation of the gentiles. That was his joy. It was the seal of his apostleship. It was his joy and crown. He came face to face with impregnable obstacles but nothing could stop him. His zeal knew no bounds **The force of focus sees no failure. It doesn't recognize defeats. It turns stumbling blocks into stepping stones. It sees problems as challenges**. When a man of focus meets obstacles, he tunnels through or round it about and move on, picking up valuable lessons in the process.

If you really desire to shape your today for a better tomorrow, you must keep your focus on your goals and aspirations. You must be dedicated and diligent in your pursuit. Your eyes must be fully focused on your vision. Your eyes must be single and concentrated on your pursuit.

> *'The light of the body is the eye: if therefore thine eye be single, thy whole body shall be full of light'*-
> Matthew 6:22

It is your sole responsibility to pursue your dreams with singleness of heart. There will be several distractions on the way. Storms of life will arise to capsize your vision boat. It is your prerogative to arise and say to the storm, peace be still. It is your job to move on in spite if odds!

Nothing could stop the Apostles from preaching the gospel of Christ in spite of obstacles and limiting factors. Nothing could stop Esther from seeing the king in order to save the Jews from the national calamity that awaited them by the sinister plot of Hamman. Nothing could stop Daniel from praying to his God. He had previously rejected the king's dainties choosing vegetables in lieu. Nothing could stop Shadrach, Meshach and Abednego from worshiping the true God.

Are you ready to shape your today for a better tomorrow? Be fully focused. **Give attention to your intention in order for it to gain expression.** Evaluate your focus and vision regularly. Everything about life is dynamic and progressive. There is room for growth. There is ample room for development.

It is not too late to make amends. You can still go to school. You can still take that development course. You can still improve your status. Do something today for a bright tomorrow. Add value to your life by adjusting the lense of your focus to fit properly. Be a man of one defined purpose. Invest and divest yourself to that one thing until light breaks forth!

CHAPTER **SIX**

God's pattern # 5: An Excellent Spirit

One virtue you can't take away from successful people is excellence. They are excellent in what they do. That was what gave me an edge during and after my engineering school in the university. I was excellent at my class works and assignments.

I told you the Italian engineering company hired me while I was still a student. Excellence was the key. God granted me the spirit of excellence like Daniel.

> *'Then this Daniel was preferred above the presidents*
> *and princes because an excellent spirit was in him...'*
> - Daniel 6:3

If you want to have an excellent spirit, stick to the word of God. That is the manual of life. Excellence is one of such instructions in the manual. You cannot be distinguished without the spirit of excellence. It is what separates the men from the boys.

Eccl. 9:10 says: 'Whatever thy hands findeth to do, do it with thy might...'

Be excellent in what you do. **Do you know how to smile? Smile so well that someone can be captivated with your smile a mile away**. Do you know how to wash the dishes? Wash them so well that dish washing can be recognized and introduced into the Olympics games. Are you good at hairdressing? Do it so well that people don't mind to travel from one state or the other to have their hair dressed in your hair salon.

Discuss, javelin and short put are some of the Olympic games. Maybe it was introduced as game because someone knew how to throw stone very well. You can carve a niche for yourself by excellent performance. Be outstanding in what you do and the world will give you a standing ovation.

A man retired from work having been an employee for several years. He was now 65. One day, he sat down under the tree, contemplating suicide. To him, it was miserable being alive. He had little or nothing to show for his several years of service.

His wife was suspicious. She was sensitive to the plight of her husband. Drawing close to him, she spoke into his ears, BUT YOU CAN COOK SO WELL! That was the magic that turned around the fortunes of this man. He went into business, dressing and selling chicken. At 84, he became a millionaire.

Your position in life is predictable when you are excellent in what you do. **Your tomorrow is bright and colorful when you are excellent in what you do today**. The world is looking for impeccable technocrats. There is room for those who have excellent spirit.

Add that midas touch. Add that flavor that introduces a difference. Be unique in your disposition. Be a first rater. Shun mediocrity in its minutest sense. Excellent people are easily spotted anywhere. They are easily noticeable. That's what distinguishes and takes them up the ladder. They cannot be at the bottom of the mountain. Their place is at the mountain top.

What makes the difference between Mr. Biggs and the restaurant at the corner of the street? Excellence: the environment, the recipe, the ambience, the packaging. The caliber of people that patronize Mr. Biggs are quite different from people who sit at the corner of the street to eat the same kind of food.

People pay more for excellence. Where a person willingly pays $10 to eat in an excellent kitchen, the same person may be reluctant to pay $1 elsewhere. The taste of excellence makes the difference. **Be excellent in your endeavors. People who have a knack for**

excellence will locate you. They will find you out and transact with you no matter what it takes to get you.

I have people I patronize because of the excellent spirit with which they operate. I have a taste for excellence. There are people like me all over the world who have a taste for excellence. If you have excellent spirit, you will attract this caliber of people.

Are you a barber? Be excellent in the discharge of your duty. Are you a seamstress? Include excellence. Be outstanding in your wood works, metal works or any creative work you are engaged in. You will be celebrated in the long run.

PS. 1:3: 'And he shall be like a tree p planted by the rivers of waters, that bringeth forth his fruits in his season; his leaf also shall not wither; and whatsoever he forth shall prosper'

God is committed to prosper your vision if you pursue it like he did in the recreation. Everything God created was good. There was nothing that was substandard in his entire handiwork. That excellent spirit is available to every believer today.

James 1:17: 'Every good gift and every perfect gift is from above, and cometh down from the father of lights, with whom there is no variableness neither shadow of turning'.

If you want to have an excellent spirit, stick to the basics; the word of God. **The word of God teaches excellence in all ramifications. It shuns laziness, mediocrity and ineptitude**. You can't be full of the word and still remain a mediocre. There is a direct affront on any vice by the virtue of excellence.

> 'Wherewithal shall a young man cleanse his way? By taking heed thereto according to thy word. With my whole heart have I sought thee: O let me not wander from thy commandments. Thy word have I hid in mine heart, that I might not sin against thee'- Psalms119: 9-11

I stuck to the word of God and the God of the word when I was still in school. When I graduated from the university, I was made the project engineer in the Italian company. Although there were bickerings here and there from older personnel, I remained the project engineer.

God gave me wisdom to solve difficult issues in the company. I rolled out my conditions of service when it became obvious that I was the lifeline in the company. I raised the bar each time. They met all my conditions. The intrigue is that God gave me solutions to the problems of the company each time they cropped up.

Be relevant in your area of jurisdiction. Be outstanding where you are and in what you do. **Create a niche for yourself. Wield the rod. Hold the ace. Be indispensable**. Let excellence permeat all your activities, secular or spiritual. You will carve a place for yourself in the ladder of achievement.

God has honoured his word above his names. The word of God is lamp unto our feet and light unto our path. It is our lifeline. The acronym, BIBLE clearly states the eternal value of God's word:

Basic
Instruction
Before
Leaving
Earth

It is our manual of life. Be a carrier of the word. Be full of the word so that when you are pressed, nothing but the word of God will ooze out of you. Let every fabric of your life be tinctured with the word. Be a carrier of the name of Jesus. If you carry Jesus, Satan and his cohorts will bow when they confront you.

Flies can only petch on a cold stove. They will get burnt when they attempt to petch on a hot stove. Be hot. Be on fire and no demon dares to harass you. **They will be too small to smite you, too weak to wear you out and too dull to dare you.**

Can a dog chase a lion? Satan is a dog. He is not a lion but roars like one. You are a lion. You are from the tribe of Judah. Jesus is the Lion of the tribe of Judah. If he is a Lion over a tribe, you are one of the lions of the tribe over which he is Lion. In other words, he is the

Lion of lions like he is the King of kings. You are one of the kings over which he is King!

Come on, rise up to who you are! **It takes a lion heart to have a lion share!** Exhibit the excellence that is peculiar with kings! Kings don't live in mediocrity. Only low lives do. They carry a personality that is above ordinary. They conduct themselves with dignity and decorum. They live a classical life. **Excellence is a mark of kingship.**

You are a king in Christ. Parade yourself like one. Live above board. Do not subject your life and vision to ridicule. Exude that aura of kings. Manifest the glory of God. Excellence is an attribute of your Father God. Let there be a touch of excellence in all you do.

You must be FAT in order to be able to display this superior quality of excellence. Even though it is part of your redemptive nature, you must grow FAT so you can unconsciously demonstrate this implicit virtue. FAT is an acronym:

F- Faithful
A- Available
T- Teachable

You must be faithful in all you do. It is a necessary prerequisite in stewardship. You are the steward of your dreams, goals and aspirations. Faithfulness must be the hallmark of your life. It must be your motto and dictum.

There are three dimensions of faithfulness you must display.

1. Faithfulness in little things
2. Faithfulness with mammon (money)
3. Faithfulness in another man's business.

If you are faithful in little things, God will commit great things to your hand. Great things start small. How faithful you are in the beginning will open you up for greater responsibilities. This is very true in ministry. It is also true in business and secular jobs.

Some people can't be trusted with money. They are good

Christians, Holy Ghost filled, tongue talkers and heaven bound. But when it comes to money matters, integrity jumps out through the window. They are not trustworthy when money is involved. If **you can't be trusted with money (material things), you will not be trusted with anointing (spiritual things).**

Faithfulness in another man's business is a prerequisite for receiving and doing your own well. The measure with which you handle another man's business is the same measure with which you will handle your own business. If you are slow, slack and sluggish with someone's business, you will be slow, slack and sluggish with yours when you eventually own one.

That's why diligent public workers always excel when they begin their business. They have cultivated the act and art of diligence, faithfulness and excellence. It's already part and parcel of them. It is a lifestyle that is unconsciously lived out. So, be faithful in little things, with mammon and in another man's business.

You must be AVAILABLE also. **God is not looking for able people. He is looking for available people.** Are you available for God to use? Can God trust you? Can God vouch for you? God could vouch for Job. He called Satan's attention to the uprightness and faithfulness of Job.

God could vouch for Mary. She was selected to be the vehicle through which Jesus would come to the world to save humanity. She was blessed among women. God could vouch for Abraham. He said in Gen. 18:19, 'For I know him that he would command his children and his household after him, and they shall keep the way of the Lord....'

Can God vouch for you? Are you available for him to use. It **is not so much of your ability but your availability. God's ability added to our responsibility gives room for possibility.** Make yourself available for God to use. Be faithful and available.

And then, you must be TEACHABLE. Some people are not teachable. They cannot be corrected. They learn very slowly. They are myopic, stereotype and conservative. They are not open to change.

Come out of your cocoon! There is a better way of doing things out there. Don't be a local champion. **<u>Learn, grow up and imbibe new things and methods. Grow with technology. Don't live in the 16th century. We are in the 21st century.</u>**

Are you teachable? Are you penitent? Are you pliable, ductile and malleable? Can God depend on you to learn and transfer knowledge to your generation? Are you inquisitive? Do you long and crave to know more of God? Do you have an insatiable hunger and thirst for God? If you are Faithful, Available and Teachable, your tomorrow is predictable. It will be glorious, gracious and great.

CHAPTER SEVEN

God's pattern # 6: Immediate Action Points

There are certain things you must do immediately. Don't procrastinate. Do it now, not tomorrow. If you have been doing them, continue and consolidate the habits until you see profitable results.

1. Have Faith. Fear is the opposite of faith. They are like two parallel lines that can never meet. Where faith exists, fear is absent and where fear rules, faith is absent. Don't be afraid. Fear is of the devil. It is a spirit you must cast out without delay.

> *'For God hath not given us the spirit of fear; but of power, and love and of a sound mind'*- 2 Timothy 1:7

<u>The spirit of fear is of the devil. Cast it out</u>. You have been given the spirit of power. You have the power to shape your today for a better tomorrow. You have the power to bind and loose. You have the power to stop the activities of Satan and his sergeants.

God laced you with a sound mind. If you are in Christ, you are a new creature. What you carry is a sound mind. Satan has no power to manipulate your mind. He does not have the capacity to twist your mind like an insane person. Your mind has imaginative and creative power. Put it to work like a jackal.

Fear not! Greater is he that's in you than he that's in the world. Don't be afraid of your bad past. Don't be haunted by past failures.

It is a trick of the devil to drag you to the past. **If he reminds you of your past, remind him of his future. That makes him mad.** He hates to know that his future eternal abode is in the lake of fire.

Fear not. There are 366 fear nots in the bible. God made provision for an extra one in case it is a leap year. **Take a daily dose of 'fearquine' and you are good to go. You will conquer obstacles, walk over the troop and bring down impregnable walls.**

Fear not. Tough times will never last.

Fear not. Ice will always thaw. You can outlive your challenges.

Fear not. That obstacle is a mere mirage and optical illusion.

Fear not. Greater is he that is in you than he that is in the world.

Fear not. The kingdom belongs to you! You are a citizen of heaven.

Fear not. Satan is already defeated. He is not a lion but a defeated dog.

Fear not. Just be armed with a vision, wisdom, plan, focus and excellence.

2. Believe in God. Trust, delight and commit yourself to God. That is the sure way you can overcome difficult situations.

'Trust in the Lord, and do good; so shalt thou dwell in the land, and verily thou shall be fed'- Psalms 37:3

'Delight thyself also in the Lord; and he shall give thee the desires of thine heart'- Psalms 37:4

'Commit thy way unto the Lord; trust also in him and he shall bring it to pass'- Psalms 37:5

The name of the Lord is a strong tower. You are safe when you run into it. God is a covenant keeping God. He is our help and strength. You can rely on him all the time.

> '*Trust in the Lord with all thine heart; and lean not unto thine own understanding*'- Proverbs 3:5

> '*They that trust in the Lord shall be as Mount Zion, which cannot be removed, but abideth for ever* '- Psalms 125:

3. Believe in yourself. If you don't believe in yourself, nobody will believe in you. Have a good self-worth. **Put a price tag on yourself or you will be priced low.** Walk tall. Walk straight and look up in hope, not down in despair. Learn to like yourself.

Are you short? Like your height. You are the best when it comes to height. Are you very tall? Like yourself the way you are. Are you dark in complexion? Are you very fair? Are you skinny or plumpy in size? You are just the best. Like yourself the way you are. Don't despise yourself. You are unique. You are specially and wonderfully made.
Believe in your ability, God's gift and grace in you.

- You are a carrier of the blessing of God. Believe it.
- You are the image and likeness of God. Believe it.
- You can do all things through Christ. Believe it.
- You can shape today for a better tomorrow. Believe it.
- You have the power to excel in your endeavor. Believe it.

At 85, Caleb believed he could possess and occupy the mountain. When Moses sent twelve spies to Canaan, only Joshua and Caleb were positive. They believed they could conquer the land. Other ten spies believed they were like grasshoppers in their own eyes.
David, as lad, believed he could kill Goliath of Gath and deliver Israel from ridicule. Abraham believed against all odds that he would

be a father of nations. He did not stagger at the promise of God through unbelief.

Believe in yourself! Thomas Edison believed in himself when everyone including his class teachers did not believe in him. A letter was given to his parents through him to advise them to withdraw him from school because he had an addled mind. They believed he would not be able to learn anything in school as a dull mind.

He believed in himself when no one gave him a chance. His achievements in the field of science proved that no one is a write off if such a person does not write off himself. He was rated the father of inventions.

The Wright brothers dreamed of a machine that would fly through the air. No one took them seriously but there is evidence all over the world that they truly had a dream which they transmuted into reality.

When Marconi dreamed of a system through which messages can be transmitted without the aid of wires, his friends had him arrested and taken to a psychopathic hospital. They believed he was out of his mind. Every radio in the world is a proof that it was Marconi's friends that were actually out of their minds.

4. Move with the progressives. Be actively involved in the kingdom business. Don't constitute a clog in the wheel. Be a solution and not part of the problem. Be an answer and not part of the questions.

There are different kinds of people. Some people are a minus in their lifestyle. They always take away and never add. They are reducing agents. Others are a plus. They add to the success story. They bring increase. They contribute to the development of the organization. There are some others that are dividers. They cause divisions. And then there are multipliers. They bring exponential growth where they are involved.

Be a progressive. Progressives are adders and multipliers. They are not reducing agents or dividers. They are meaningful contributors. Their involvement always effect a change. They bring about multiplier effect. Never be a minus to the kingdom. Be a plus. Never be a divider. Be a multiplier.

5. Be positive in all your undertakings. All things are possible to those who believe. Be a positive thinker. Be a possibility thinker. Think forward. Think big. Think positive. Think possible.

Luke 1:37: 'For with God nothing shall be impossible'

6. Remove distractions. Don't let anything clog the wheel of your progress. Remove the specks and logs. Remove negative habits. Roll away the stone. That was the first instruction Jesus gave Mary and Martha beside the grave of Lazarus.

Roll away the stone that hinders the fulfillment of your destiny. **Roll away obstacles that are within; obstacles only you can roll away**. Settle sin issues. God is holy. He requires us to live in holiness. You are the righteousness of God in Christ Jesus. Live right. Talk right. Behave right.

7. Go for the best. Don't settle down for crumbs. Don't be a second rater. There are certain myths you may have to throw out of your life. They are lies from the pit of hell. You will be deceived if you continue to believe them.

'All fingers are not equal'. It is a lie of the devil. Don't underrate yourself thinking others are more qualified or others are better. You can achieve just anything others can.

'A fool at 40 is a fool forever'. This is a lie of the devil. All hope is not gone because you are more than 40 years of age. You can still shine at 50. You can still break new grounds at 60. Rather believe that life begins at 40 instead of a fool at 40 is a fool forever.

'A bird at hand is worth two in the bush'. This is a lie from the pit of hell. You can let go something for another. Sometimes if the bed at hand does not fly away, you may never have the first to catch a bigger one. And what you are holding may withhold you from receiving what is being stretched out to you!

'Look before you leap'. This is also a lie. People who look before they leap never leap. They look and keep looking, procrastinating and contemplating in the process. Don't look before you leap. Leap after you look!

I commend you unto God, our Father and Creator who owns tomorrow. May he send you help from his sanctuary and strengthen you out of Zion to shape your today for a better tomorrow. May his grace be sufficient for you in the process. May you excel. May you break forth and breakthrough to the glory of God. Amen.

Printed in the United States
By Bookmasters